yellow e

Running the Silk Road

丝路长征

By PAUL SIRETT
Conceived and directed by DAVID TSE KA-SHING
Designed by YOON BAE

First performed at the Northern Stage, Newcastle on 28 May 2008

Performed with English surtitles
Presented in association with Beijing Opera Theatre and Watford Palace Theatre
Sponsored by China Now

Running the Silk Road
by Paul Sirett
Conceived and directed by David Tse Ka-Shing

CAST (IN ORDER OF APPEARANCE)

Ken	Nick Chee Ping Kellington
Jahid	Saraj Chaudhry
Dina, Iranian Woman	Betsabeh Emran
Wei, Chinese Man 2	Chia Kuei Chen
Xi, Nü Ch'ou	Gongxin Lan
Lei Shen, Tajik Man, Chinese Man 1	Shen Feng
Yü, Yi, Iranian Man	Yanzhong Huang
Writer	Paul Sirett
Director	David Tse Ka-Shing
Dramaturges	Philippe Cherbonnier, Brigid Larmour & David Tse Ka-Shing
Designer	Yoon Bae
Composer and Sound Designer	Suki Mok
Lighting Designer	Douglas Kuhrt
Translator & Surtitles	Eko Fiza Laukaban
Assistant Director & Interpreter	Liya Wu
Production Manager	Jim Leaver
Company Stage Manager	Anna Kerr
Deputy Stage Manager	Roshni Savjani
Assistant Stage Manager	Jennifer Western
Puppets	Blind Summit
Additional Puppets	Yoon Bae, Anna Kerr, Jennifer Western
Costume Makers	Sunwoo Chun, Eunju Chong, Chihiro Kokubu
Wardrobe Assistant	Holly Marie Dench
Marketing	Spark Arts Marketing: 020 7655 4460, ben@sparkuk.com
Press	Arthur Leone: 020 7637 2994, anna@arthurleone.com
Education Associates	Kumiko Mendl (director), Kathy Hall, Sinman Yue, Joanna Qiu

Special thanks to Yellow Earth's funders and sponsors for this production:
Arts Council England, China Now, Shaftesbury plc, Sir David Tang, British Council CtC, Good Earth Group, Lupton Travel.

Shaftesbury PLC

BIOGRAPHIES

Paul Sirett *Writer*

Paul is a playwright and dramaturg. Productions of Paul's plays include *The Big Life* (Theatre Royal Stratford East & West End), *Lush Life* (Live Theatre, Newcastle), *Rat Pack Confidential* (Nottingham Playhouse/Bolton Octagon & West End), *A Night In Tunisia*, *Worlds Apart*, *Crusade*, *Jamaica House* (all Theatre Royal Stratford East) and *Skaville* (Bedlam, Edinburgh & Soho Theatre). Radio plays include *Vissi D'Arte*, *Hellhound On My Trial* and *Eva Bergen* (all BBC Radio 4). Awards include *Vissi D'Arte* (LBC/LAB New radio Playwrights - Winner, New York Radio Festival – Best Play & Best Writer, Prix Italia – Special Commendation), *World Apart* (Thames Television Theatre Writers Scheme – Best Play), *Rat Pack Confidential* (City Life – Best production), *The Big Life* (Olivier Awards, Evening Standard, TMA Awards – nomination for Best Musical). Paul was Literary manager at Soho Theatre from 1994-2001 and Dramaturg at the Royal Shakespeare Company from 2001-2005. Paul is currently International Associate at Soho Theatre.

David Tse Ka-Shing
Director and Artistic Director

Trained at Rose Bruford and Leicester Haymarket. He studied Beijing Opera movement with Lee Siu Wah and during *M. Butterfly* with Jamie Guan. Directing for Yellow Earth includes: *King Lear* (Shanghai Arts Festival / RSC Complete Works, UK tour); *Nightingale* (Hong Kong Arts Festival, UK tour); *Chinese Two-Step* (Trafalgar Sqare); *58* (UK tour); *Lear's Daughters* (UK tour); *Butcher's Skin* (UK & Denmark); *Play to Win* (Sainsbury's Checkout Award, Soho & UK tour); *New Territories* (Time Out Critics' Choice, UK tour) and *Animal Farm* (Denmark); *Kensuke's Kingdom* (Polka); *Dance & the Railroad* and *House of Sleeping Beauties* (Leicester Haymarket). New writing and adaptations include: *King Lear*, *Nightingale*, *Play to Win*, *New Territories*; *Snow Lion* (Polka); *Magic Paintbrush* (TMA Award nominee) and *Old Woman & the Beggar* (Radio 3). Extensive acting and presenting credits include a groundbreaking series on Radio 4, *Beyond the Takeaway*. Awards: Rose Bruford Fellowship, Windrush Arts Award. In 2004, Yellow Earth won the Pearl Arts Award. *Running the Silk Road* is his last production for Yellow Earth, before embarking on a freelance career. David is also Creative Director of Chinatown Arts Space (www.chinatownartsspace.com).

Yoon Bae
Set and Costume Designer

Yoon is a British-Korean designer, currently based in London. Yoon studied at CSSD, and the Slade School, UCL. Previously with Yellow Earth Theatre, Yoon designed *The Whisper of a Leaf Falling*, *Dogs* and *Getting Married*. In the West End, she is associate designer on *Gone with the Wind*. She designed *Three Thousand Troubled Threads* for Edinburgh International Festival and *Picasso's Women* for ATG. In Korea, she designed an award winning musical, *Music in My Heart, Closer* at Seoul Arts Centre and the musical *The Full Monty*. She has worked extensively in the UK designing new plays including *Wounds to the Face* for Howard Barker's Wrestling School, to *Private Lives* in Scotland and *Live Bed Show* with Bob Carlton for a major national tour (www.yoonbae.com).

Suki Mok
Composer and Sound Designer

Suki graduated from the Welsh School of Architecture with a scholarship before moving on to the renowned Powerhouse music college where he graduated with a degree from The Guitar Institute. He has since played with various bands and artists across the London gig circuit, formed the

Chinese Music Collective (a non-profit organisation supporting up and coming Chinese musicians), and taught at workshops, clinics and privately at his project studio. Suki currently works extensively as a session musician, composer and producer. He scores music for film, commercial video, theatre and writes and produces for bands and singers. He is currently writing his debut album due to be released in 2009.

Douglas Kuhrt *Lighting Designer*

Doug is proud to be working on David Tse's final production for Yellow Earth as artistic director. Doug and David have been working with each other now for ten years! Doug is currently lighting Lee Hall's new play *The Pitmen Painters* at the National Theatre. Other shows include: *There's Something About Simmy*, *The Deranged Marriage* (Rifco); *King Lear* (Yellow Earth, Shanghai); *The Nightingale* (Yellow Earth, Hong Kong); *Tom, Dick & Harry* (Duke of York's); *Zipp!* (Duchess); *The Beast Market* (Chol); *The Talisman* (Drum, Plymouth); *Stamping, Shouting and Screaming Home* (Polka); *Stuart Little* (Bromley); *Fascinating Aida* (Haymarket); *Home and Beauty* (Lyric); *Party Piece* (Windsor); *Aladdin* (Liverpool Everyman); *Dick Whittington* (Qdos); *Dreaming*, *The Hobbit* (Queens); *Naked Justice* (West Yorkshire Playhouse).

Nick Chee Ping Kellington *Actor*

Physical actor and musician. Theatre credits include: *Cloudcuckooland*, *The Onassis Project*, *Cruel Sea*, (Everyman Liverpool); *The Smallest Person* (Nominated Best Actor, Edinburgh Fringe, The Stage Awards) and *The Adventures of the Stoneheads* (Trestle Theatre); *Grimm Tales*, (The Dukes Playhouse); *The Three Musketeers*, *Backwater*, *B.L.T* and *The Bank* *Job*, (Spike Theatre); *Robin Hood*, (Ophaboom Theatre); and *Moby Dick*, (Walk the Plank/Kaboodle) Co-production. Television: has recently appeared as a Sontaron Warrior in *Dr Who* and plays Igglepiggle in the Children's BAFTA Award-winning series *In The Night Garden*.

Saraj Chaudhry
Actor

Trained Guildford School of Acting. Theatre work includes: AL (Double / Littlewood) in *A Disappearing Number*, (Theatre De Complicite, Barbican – Best Play: Olivier Awards, Evening Standard Awards, Critics Circle Theatre Awards); Ashish in *White Open Spaces* (Soho) nominated for **South Bank Show Award**; Bobby in *Players* (WYP); Nitin in *Indi-Yaar* (Young Vic/Paines Plough); Pablo in *Penguin Suits & Sequins* (Waterman's); Arab Boy in *Murder* (Gate); Dan in *Closer* (Cochrane); Soranzo in *Tis Pity She's A Whore* (Guildford Yvonne Arnaud). Films include: Sonny in *Bend It Like Beckham*, Tariq in *Bollywood Queen*, Thomas in *Check Mate*. Fight choreographer: *Big Game Hunting*. TV: George Cartwright (regular), *Adventure*, Vijay Sud – *The Bill*, Nokol in *Adventure Inc* (HBO/Sky TV); Dev in *Casualty*, Abu in *Monkey Dust*, *Paradise Heights* and Jailor in *NCS* (all BBC).

Betsabeh Emran
Actress

Betsabeh began her career as an actress in 1997 at the Barnes Youth Theatre under Ed Cottrell. She completed a degree in Music and Drama with First Class honours in 2001. Her theatre credits include work with Frantic Assembly, Rambert Dance Company, Told by an Idiot, Oxford Stage Company,

Birmingham Repertory Theatre and the Royal Court. Betsabeh recently completed a short film, *Death of a Knife Salesman*, directed by Josh Wroe for the NFT. Her film and television credits include Matthew Vaughn's *Layer Cake*, Stephen Hopkins' *The Life and Death of Peter Sellers*, and numerous credits with BBC Television and Radio.

Chia-Kuei Chen
Actor

Trained at Taipei National University of the Arts and at Drama Centre London and gained a MFA in Acting and a MA in Performance respectively. He has been working in theatre, film and TV in Taiwan and here in the UK as well. His recent credits include the short film *Lies* directed by Stuart Urban, TV commercial *Lucky Boat Noodles* directed by Jackson Pat. He has also directed short films, including *Homeless* (director and actor), which was chosen to represent the UK at the Berlin Talent Campus 2007.

Gongxin Lan *Actress*

Gongxin Lan graduated from Qindao Art School, China in 2000. Her expertise is in singing Beijing Opera, in addition to which she is skilled in Opera dancing and movement. In 2002, she appeared in the *Elegant and Flourishing Age* jointly presented by CCTV and China Traditional Opera College. She was cast in *Du Siniang* (Beijing Opera) and also in *Famous Arias of Famous Artists*, singing opera arias at the Chinese Autumn Festival held by CCTV. Gongxin has performed at the Beijing Opera Art Festival and joined the Beijing Opera Theatre of Beijing in 2004, with whom she has performed in many cities throughout China.

Shen Feng *Actor*

Shen Feng joined the Beijing Opera Theatre of Beijing in 2004 just after graduation. Talented in acrobatics, martial arts and Beijing Opera spears and swords, in 2005 he took part in the grand performance for World 500 Enterprises. He has performed in *The Real and Fake Monkey King* in Hong Kong, Japan and Thailand, and has appeared extensively in many high profile productions with the Beijing Opera Theatre.

Yanzhong Huang
Actor

Graduated from Beijing Traditional Classical Opera School in 1985 and is especially known as a Wusheng actor. Extremely skilled at singing, martial arts, Beijing Opera Theatre spears and sword fighting and clowning skills, leading roles include *Fire Attack to Yu Hong*, *Generals from Yang Family*, *Golden Beach*, *Qin Xianglian* and many other productions. Awards include: 1987 screen prize for the National Beijing Opera TV Championship Contest; 1988 excellent performing prize in the Traditional Operas Performing; 1992 excellent performing for New Programs performed by the National Youth Beijing Opera Troupes; 1994 silver prize for Mei Lanfang Golden Championship Contest. He has toured to Korea, England, Italy, Austria, Germany, Japan, the United States, Canada and Malaysia.

Liya Wu
Assistant Director / Interpreter

Liya trained in LISPA (London), and now focuses on writing and directing. Her first play, *Mr Whippendale…* (About two soldiers on an island) was selected by the English Theatre of Bruges to perform in Belgium for two weeks. She is now working on her second play, *Cherry or Burgundy?* The concurrent themes in her writing at the moment are death and abandoned babies. Before London, she was an industry reporter on CCTV cameras in Taiwan where she also co-directed a documentary, *Lu Man-Mei*, about the Taiwanese 'comfort women' used by the Japanese army during the Second World War. Being conveniently fluent in three languages, she swears in Taiwanese, fights in Mandarin Chinese and argues in English (www.liya.burntmango.org).

Jim Leaver *Production Manager*

Theatre: *Rent*, *Little Shop of Horrors*, *Who's Afraid of Virginia Woolf?*, *One Flew Over the Cuckoo's Nest*, *Medea*, *Dangerous Corner* (West End); *Mouse Queen* (Broadway); *The Good Hope*, National Theatre; *Martha Josie & the Chinese Elvis* (Birmingham Rep); *Sugar Mummies* and *My Name is Rachel Corrie*, (Royal Court); *The Three Sisters* and *Single Spies* (Theatre Royal Bath). Opera: *Eugene Onegin*, *Lulu*, *The Barber of Seville* (ENO); *Coronation of Poppea*, *Tolemeo*, *Die Fledermaus*, *Rape of Lucretia*, *Turn of the Screw*, *Revenge of the Carmelites*, *Cosi Fan Tutte*, (RCM); *The Magic Flute*, (RAM). Circus: *Romeo and Juliet* (Playhouse Theatre); *The Birds*, National Theatre; *Jettix*, (Generating Company); *The Little Mermaid*, (Sphinx Theatre Company); *Loser* (Company FZ),

Anna Kerr *Company Stage Manager*

Anna's career began at York's Grand Opera House on shows including *Annie*, *Wizard of Oz* and *Wind in the Willows*. Anna worked for New Pantomime Productions in 2000 on *Cinderella* and *Mother Goose*. She was Project Manager in Malaysia for Raleigh International in 2004 returning for a National Tour of *Lord of the Flies*. Anna has worked extensively for Little Angel Theatre, Pilot Theatre Company, Half Moon Young People's Theatre, Hull Truck and Trestle Theatre Company. Most recently working on *The Wizard of Oz* and *Cyrano de Bergerac* at the Haymarket Theatre Basingstoke and *The Internationalist* at The Gate Theatre.

Roshni Savjani
Deputy Stage Manager

Roshni worked extensively at the Bridewell Theatre and Theatre Royal Stratford East as a member of their resident Stage Management teams. She has worked both the Edinburgh and Adelaide Fringe Festivals and her most recent credits include, *I Saw Myself* directed by Howard Barker, *World's End* at Trafalgar Studios, *Two Way Mirror* at London's Theatre Museum, *Babel Junction* at Hackney Empire and various projects at Soho Theatre. Roshni has toured with Rifco Arts on their sell-out national tours of *Deranged Marriage*, *There's Something About Simmy* and *Meri Christmas*.

Jennifer Western
Assistant Stage Manager

After gaining an Upper Second Class degree in Theatre Studies in 2004 Jennifer sought work experience in London as an Assistant Stage Manager and was fortunate to gain West End experience on *As You Like It* in 2005. In 2006 she went on to stage manage several London Fringe productions at The Hen & Chickens and The Pleasance theatres. Jennifer has been working professionally in Stage Management since September 2006. During this time she has worked at a number of theatre companies including The Sheffield Theatres, Rifco Arts, The Haymarket Basingstoke and The Wrestling School.

yellow earth theatre

Yellow Earth was established in 1995 by five British East Asian performers with the aim of raising the profile and standing of British East Asian theatre. The company has won many awards including the *Pearl Award for Creative Award* (2004), the *Windrush Award* (Arts Achievement Award to David Tse Ka-shing, 2004) and *Sainsbury's Checkout Theatre Award* (1999).

David Tse Ka-Shing is Artistic Director and one of the Founder Members. A key artistic partner in the first six years was Tom Wu (Movement Director), who enabled a body of work to be created that explored East Asian physical theatre. The other Founder Members, Kumiko Mendl, Veronica Needa and Kwong Loke, were joined by Philippe Cherbonnier, Literary Associate, marking a shift towards East Asian text and new writing, while retaining a keen interest in East Asian physical theatre.

Yellow Earth now regularly produces British East Asian work that uses multimedia, East Asian physical theatre and bilingual text. Its audiences are diverse and attract a relatively large percentage of British East Asians. Yellow Earth is the UK's flagship British East Asian national touring theatre company, revenue funded by Arts Council England (London). Yellow Earth produces touring productions which have found an international market and runs the UK's only international East Asian play reading festival and training schemes for emerging East Asian writers, directors and youth and community groups.

YELLOW EARTH THEATRE

Artistic Director   **David Tse Ka-Shing**
General Manager   **Susannah Kraft**
Education and Outreach Associate   **Kumiko Mendl**
Literary Associate   **Philippe Cherbonnier**
Financial Administrator   **Abby-Lee Widger**
Administrator and Marketing Assistant   **Ann Cross**
Development and Fundraising   **Cecilia Finet**
Intern   **Belinda Tang**

PATRON:
Sir David Tang

BOARD:
Daniel Gilsenan, Ming Kong, Stephen Midlane, Wah-Yin Rixon

Thanks
Yellow Earth would like to thank: Kathy Hall; Opera Singer image: supplied by London Jing Kun Opera Association and photographed by Jessica Hall; Hiker image: supplied by Getty Images and photographed by Paul Edmonson; the Barbican Centre; The British Council in Beijing; Matt Duggan (magic); Sasha Yevtushenko, Jitka Suchoparkova (Russian); Tony Western (prop graphics); Noi Kuan (interpreter); Professor Anne Birrell, Rifco and Polka Theatre

PREVIOUS PRODUCTIONS

Typhoon Live (2007)   **Dogs** by Elangovan, directed by Kwong Loke
Getting Married by Yi Kang-baek, directed by Philippe Cherbonnier

King Lear (2006)   by Shakespeare, adapted and directed by David K.S. Tse

Chinese Two-Step:
1925 - 2005 (2005)   by Andy Cheung, directed by David K.S. Tse

The Nightingale (2005)   by Hans Christian Andersen, adapted and directed by David K.S. Tse

58 (2004)   by Philippe Cherbonnier, directed by David K.S.Tse

Festival for the Fish (2004)   by Yu Miri, directed by Kwong Loke

Lear's Daughters (2003)   by Elaine Feinstein & The Women's Theatre Group, directed by David K.S. Tse

The Butcher's Skin (2002)   by Luu Quang Vu, directed by David K.S. Tse

Face (2002)   by Veronica Needa, directed by Shu-Wing Tang

Rashomon (2001)   by Philippe Cherbonnier, directed by Kwong Loke, Kumiko Mendl & David K.S. Tse

Play to Win (2000)   written and directed by David K.S. Tse

Blue Remembered Hills (1999)   by Dennis Potter, directed by David Glass

The Whisper of a Leaf Falling (1998)   written and directed by Philippe Cherbonnier

Behind the Chinese Take Away (1997)   by the Company, directed by Erika Tan & David K.S. Tse

New Territories (1996)   written and directed by David K.S. Tse

SILK WEB

Silk Web is a Youth Performance project with secondary school students from Longdean School, Hemel Hempstead, Kidbrooke School, SE London and Charles Edward Brooke School, S. London. The students will be working with either a professional Chinese dancer, musician or Beijing Opera storyteller to explore the ancient myths from *Running the Silk Road*. They will come together for performances at Watford Palace Theatre and at the Pit, Barbican Centre. 19 June 2008 at Watford Palace Theatre, 26 June 2008 at the Pit, Barbican Centre. *Silk Web has been completely funded by China Now*

For more information or to join our mailing list
Yellow Earth Theatre, 18 Rupert Street, London W1D 6DE
T: 020 7734 5988   F: 020 7287 3141   E: admin@yellowearth.org
www.yellowearth.org
To join our e-mailing list, please visit: **www.yellowearth.org/mailinglist**
Registered in England no.3045132
Registered charity no.1047991
VAT no. 740148849

Yellow Earth Theatre
Running the Silk Road
Tour dates

NEWCASTLE
Northern Stage
27 – 31 May, 8pm
Box Office 0191 230 5151
Book online www.northernstage.co.uk

LIVERPOOL
Liverpool Everyman
3 - 7 June, 7.45pm; 4 June 1.30pm & 7 June 2pm
Box Office 0151 709 4776
Book online www.everymanplayhouse.com

BURY ST EDMUNDS
Theatre Royal, Bury St Edmunds
10 June, 7.30pm; 11 June 2pm & 7.30pm
(Matinee Wed 2.30pm)
Box Office 01284 769505
Book online www.theatreroyal.org

EXETER
Northcott Theatre Exeter
12 – 14 June, 7.30pm
Box Office 01392 493 493
Book online www.exeternorthcott.co.uk

WATFORD
Watford Palace Theatre
17 – 21 June, 7.45pm; 18 June, 2.30pm & 21 June 3pm
Box Office 01923 225671
Book online www.watfordtheatre.co.uk

LONDON
The Pit, Barbican Centre
24 – 28 June, 7.45pm
Box Office 020 7638 8891
Book online www.barbican.org.uk

COMING SOON…

Typhoon V: Make sure you catch the new season of East Asian plays in the next Typhoon festival, autumn 2008 at Soho Theatre, London. Contact Yellow Earth for further information: admin@yellowearth.org or visit www.yellowearth.org

RUNNING THE SILK ROAD

First published in 2008 by Oberon Books Ltd
521 Caledonian Road, London N7 9RH
Tel: 020 7607 3637 / Fax: 020 7607 3629
e-mail: info@oberonbooks.com
www.oberonbooks.com

Copyright © Paul Sirett 2008

Paul Sirett is hereby identified as author of this play in accordance with section 77 of the Copyright, Designs and Patents Act 1988. The author has asserted his moral rights.

All rights whatsoever in this play are strictly reserved and application for performance etc. should be made before commencement of rehearsal to Independent Talent Group, Oxford House, 76 Oxford Street, London W1D 1BS. No performance may be given unless a licence has been obtained, and no alterations may be made in the title or the text of the play without the author's prior written consent.

This book is sold subject to the condition that it shall not by way of trade or otherwise be circulated without the publisher's consent in any form of binding or cover or circulated electronically other than that in which it is published and without a similar condition including this condition being imposed on any subsequent purchaser.

A catalogue record for this book is available from the British Library.

ISBN: 978-1-84002-857-7

Cover photographs by Paul Edmonson/Getty Images (hiker) and Jessica Hall / London Jing Kun Opera Association (opera singer).

Printed in Great Britain by Antony Rowe, Chippenham.

Characters

Present Day Characters

KEN

JAHID

DINA

WEI

XI

Main Mythological Characters

LEI SHEN

NÜ CH'OU CHIH SHIH

YÜ

YI

All other parts played by members of the company or enacted using puppets/shadow puppets, etc.

All dialogue in bold type is spoken in Mandarin.

A / indicates overlapping dialogue.

All references in the footnotes are from the *Shan Hai Jing* (*The Classic of Mountains and Seas*) unless otherwise stated.

SCENE 1

June 2007.
KEN enters and stands at a lectern.

KEN: Good evening. Thank you for coming. My name is Kenneth Fung. I am going to talk to you tonight about the *Shan Hai Jing, The Classic of Mountains and Seas.* The *Shan Hai Jing* is over two thousand years old and the stories it contains are at least that old again. Book One begins: 'The first mountain of the Classic of the Southern Mountains is called Mount Magpie. It stands over the West Sea. There is an animal here, shaped like an ape with white ears. When it walks, it crouches, when it runs, it runs like a man. Its name is Sheng-sheng. He who eats it will be a good runner…' a good runner…

SCENE 2

June 2007.
Students' Union bar, London. KEN, DINA, JAHID.

JAHID: This man goes into a bar / and he's…

DINA: Jahid –

JAHID: No, no, it's a good one this. He's sitting there drinking his beer and eating some nuts when he hears this really sexy voice, 'You've got lovely eyes!' The bloke looks round, but he can't see no-one, the bar's completely empty apart from him, so he goes back to his beer. A minute later, he hears the same voice, 'You're very handsome!' He looks round again, but he still can't see where the voice is coming from. He turns back to his beer, and the voice is there again, 'You're really very, very attractive!' He jumps up, looks everywhere – nothing! Well, by now the bloke is desperate so he turns to the barman, 'What's going on?' he asks. 'Oh, you don't want to worry about that,' says the barman, 'it's the peanuts – they're complimentary.'

DINA groans. KEN doesn't respond.

(*To KEN.*) …complimentary…

Still no reaction from KEN.

Forget it.

DINA: (*To KEN.*) How did your lecture go?

KEN shrugs.

Is there something wrong? Ken?

KEN: Me and Xi split up.

DINA: Oh…

JAHID: Shit.

KEN: Don't tell Wei.

JAHID: What?

KEN: Don't tell my cousin.

DINA: Why?

KEN: Because I don't want the family to know yet.

DINA: When did this happen?

KEN: Last Saturday. I haven't slept for a week.

JAHID: I thought you looked rough.

KEN: Thanks.

DINA: Why didn't you say anything?

KEN: Because I thought she'd…because… I've been trying to patch things –

WEI enters with drinks.

Thanks.

DINA: (*To WEI.*) How long are you in London for?

WEI: How…?

DINA: How long? London. How long are you staying?

WEI: **She wants to know how long I'm staying in London?**

KEN: Yes.

WEI: **I haven't decided yet.**

KEN: He hasn't decided yet.

DINA: Are you here on holiday?

WEI: I learn English.

DINA: Right. What do you do in China?

KEN: He doesn't live in China, he lives in Africa.

WEI: I live in Congo. Congo-Brazzaville.

DINA: Really? What do you do there?

WEI looks to KEN for help.

KEN: Wei works for his Dad's timber company. They've only been out there since 2000. They've made a fortune. He's taking a year out to do some travelling and learn English before taking up a job as some kind of senior executive in the company.

DINA: I think it's appalling how China exploits Africa's natural resources.

WEI: **What?**

KEN: Shall we change the subject?

JAHID: (*To KEN.*) So is the wedding off?

Pause.

WEI: **Your wedding is off?**

KEN: Thanks, Jahid. Yes, the wedding is off.

WEI: **Do your parents know?**

KEN: No. I haven't told my parents yet.

DINA: What happened?

KEN: I don't want / to talk…

DINA: It's out now, Ken. You might as well tell us.

KEN: I asked if she'd mind moving the date to next year.

DINA: Why?

KEN: So that I could finish the research for my doctorate. She thought I was making an excuse to stop getting married, but I wasn't, I just want to finish my research.

JAHID: On that mad book?

KEN: It's not a 'mad book'!

DINA: What did she say?

KEN: She said I could forget getting married at all if that was the case.

DINA: And that was it?

KEN: She said I obviously didn't care about her. I told her she was being irrational. Then she started on about how she was tired of playing second best to my research, how I never do anything except read and make notes. I tried to explain. I have a routine. I get up at six, I go jogging, I shower, I have breakfast, I write in the mornings, I have lunch, in the afternoon I go to the library to do my research, in the evening I eat dinner, after which I read more broadly on the subject of Chinese Mythology or world geography, I go to bed at eleven. On Tuesdays, Thursdays and Saturdays I work the afternoon shift at Starbucks. It's a set routine. It works. If I can continue like this for the next six months I'll really be getting somewhere.

DINA: What did she say?

KEN: She said I had obsessive-compulsive disorder.

JAHID laughs.

KEN: What?

JAHID: She's got a point.

KEN: I haven't!

JAHID: Come off it. You have a panic attack if someone rearranges your pencils in the wrong order.

DINA: Jahid –

JAHID: I'm sorry, it's just…Ken, look, don't take this the wrong way but you can't tell the person you're about to marry that you think some crappy old book is more important / than she is…

KEN: That wasn't what I / said…

JAHID: Where's the romance? Where's the passion?

DINA: You're a fine one to speak.

JAHID: I'm just trying to point out that…that…

KEN: I'm boring.

JAHID: No. Yes.

DINA: Ken is not boring.

JAHID: His idea of fun is going through all his books to see which one has the longest footnote.

DINA: Don't be stupid.

KEN: I did that.

JAHID: I rest my case.

KEN: I just want her back, that's all.

JAHID: Yeah, she's amazing.

DINA: Is there nothing you can do?

KEN: I've been trying. Every day. I told her I was sorry. In the end I said I'd stick to the original date. But then she… going on about how I don't care about the real world and things that are happening to real people. How there are people dying and all I'm interested in is some book from two thousand years ago. I do care. I do…It's just…I never do anything. I just sit there and read. I am boring. I don't like it if my routine gets disrupted. I hate leaving anything to chance. I should be more passionate. I know I should… I've screwed up… I know I… I love her so much…

DINA: I'll talk to her.

KEN: No –

DINA: I'll / talk to her…

KEN: You can't. You can't.

DINA: Why?

KEN: She's gone to Guangdong. To China. Where they've had all the floods.

JAHID: What, like in Worcestershire?

KEN: Not exactly. Sixty-six people died.

JAHID: I never knew that.

DINA: That's because you never watch the news.

JAHID: (*Indicating KEN.*) He never watches the news.

KEN: It wasn't on the news. Xi was furious. Someone gets a wet garden in Kidderminster and it's all over the six o'clock news. Over sixty people die in flash floods in China and no one takes a blind bit of notice.

WEI: **She has relatives in Guangdong?**

KEN: No. She doesn't have any relatives there. She works for a Chinese charity. They've got a warehouse in Guangzhou. They only opened it a couple of months ago to help with drought relief.

JAHID: Hold on, how can you have a flood and a drought at the same time?

KEN: It happens.

DINA: I'll call her.

KEN: No. Dina… She wants time to think, she doesn't want anyone contacting her. It's up to me… I have to do something. I have to show her I care… I have to show her that I'm not some obsessive-compulsive who's frightened to leave the library… I've had an idea, that's why I wanted to see you. I wondered if-if…if you'd help? I want to raise money for Xi's charity. As much as I can.

DINA: What are you going to do?

KEN: A sponsored run.

WEI: **A sponsored run?**

KEN: I run every day. I've done the London Marathon the last two years. I took ten minutes, thirty-one seconds off my time this year.

DINA: A sponsored run?

KEN: Yes.

DINA: How far?

KEN: About five thousand miles.

JAHID: Five…! What are you going to do – run round the M25 for the next three years?

KEN: I'm going to run to China.

JAHID: Wh-!

DINA: China?

WEI: **China.**

KEN: That's why I want your help. I need a support team.

JAHID: You need a therapist!

DINA: There is the small matter of my MA.

KEN: You can defer it for a year.

DINA: They won't let me.

KEN: I've spoken to your tutor. She's cool about it.

DINA: You've –

KEN: Just to sound her out. Hypothetically.

DINA: You could have asked me.

KEN: I didn't mention your name, I just asked if someone was to…you know… She said it would be fine.

DINA: Why me?

KEN: You're my friend. And I thought we could take your car?

DINA: It's a second-hand Daewoo Lanos. It only got through its last MOT because Frankenstein at the garage fancies me.

KEN: Please, Dina… (*Takes out a large file from his briefcase.*) Look, I've worked it out. The run starts here in Turkey and ends in Beijing.

DINA takes the file and reads.

JAHID: Turkey?

KEN: I'm going to run along the Silk Road. Me and Xi were supposed to be travelling along the Silk Road for our honeymoon. Xian. Dunhuang…

WEI: **The cave paintings there are amazing.**

KEN: … It's an ancient trading route between east and west, west and east – depending on which way you're going. So I thought… And here's the brilliant bit. If I run a half marathon every day I could do it in just over a year and / arrive in…

JAHID: A year?

KEN: Yes. And arrive in Beijing just before the Olympic Games at the same time as the Olympic torch.

JAHID: What's so good about that?

KEN: I'll be carrying an alternative torch with a green flame, a symbol of global warming.

JAHID: You don't care about global warming.

KEN: I do.

DINA: You're serious about this aren't you?

KEN: Yes.

DINA studies KEN's file again.

JAHID: You can't run that / far –

KEN: Serious marathon runners run up to a hundred and fifty miles / a week…

JAHID: Yes, but you've / never run that far –

KEN: Jahid… Jahid… Jahid… Okay. Jahid. Jahid. Look: (*Pause.*) I don't run a hundred and fifty miles a week, but I don't have to. A half marathon is just over thirteen miles / if I can…

JAHID: It's too far.

KEN: There was this… I can't remember his name. This American ultramarathon runner who ran fifty consecutive marathons…twen – over twenty-six miles every day for fifty days in fifty different states. And / there was a…and…

JAHID: It's still not five / thousand miles though is it…

KEN: Listen to me. Jahid… Jahid… Listen! There was an eight-year-old…an eight-year-old Chinese girl who ran over two thousand miles to celebrate Beijing getting the Olympics.

WEI: **I've heard about that.**

DINA: Yes and her Father got accused of child abuse for making her / do it…

KEN: She ran over two / thousand…

JAHID: Yes, yes.

WEI: **What about finance?**

JAHID: What?

KEN: Wei is asking about finance. I don't know. Yet. I want to appoint a fundraiser. We've got a few weeks to work something out. I wouldn't have to leave until next month.

DINA: It goes through Iran.

KEN: What? Yes.

DINA: You know I've got family there?

JAHID: I thought they'd all left.

DINA: No. God! You'd never believe we went out for two years.

JAHID: Axis of evil.

DINA: You're the scary Sunni Muslim here, not me.

JAHID: Scary Sunni Muslim comedian if you don't mind.

DINA: Scary Sunni Muslim bad comedian with material that was out of date twenty years ago.

KEN: Can we focus?

DINA: I've never been to Iran. Mum's always been dead set against it.

KEN: Are you going to come?

DINA: I don't know / Ken –

KEN: Say you'll think about it.

DINA: I'll think about it.

KEN hugs DINA.

How much do you want to raise?

KEN: I don't know. Fiver a mile. Twenty-five grand.

DINA: You could raise a lot more than that.

KEN: Great. I thought we could set up a website for donations. Jahid…? You know all about that. Would you help me set up a website?

JAHID: Yes, all right.

KEN: Fantastic. And what about…? You going to come? You've got time.

JAHID: I've got a job.

KEN: You work at *Phones 4 U*.

JAHID: And your point is?

DINA: Come on, Jahid. You always said that one day you wanted to travel.

JAHID: Yes, to Miami, to Goa, to Buenos Aires.

KEN: I need you there to annoy me. I need you to keep going on about how I'm never going to make it.

JAHID: You won't make it.

KEN: See! That's is exactly what I mean. Do you have any idea how irritating that is?

JAHID: No libraries. No musty old books. No shuffling old men in thick glasses with corduroy jackets covered in dandruff.

KEN: I'll cope. Are you going to come?

KEN holds out his hand, DINA takes it. Beat. JAHID takes their hands. They all look at him.

WEI: I come with you.

KEN: Yes?

WEI nods.

WEI: (*To KEN.*) **I will be your backer.**

KEN: Wei said he'll be our backer.

WEI: **My father said I should get out and see the world and have an adventure. What could be better?**

KEN: He says his father told him to get out and see the world and have an adventure.

WEI: Cheers!

ALL: Cheers!

SCENE 3

August 2007. Running sequence. Turkey. Turkish/Kurdish music. KEN is running with the alternative Olympic torch – a green flame.

KEN: I'm running along this parched road. Past these staring people. Past these Turkish policemen and curious Kurdish children. Past this church. This mosque. These dusty cars. Beneath this August sun. I'm running. I don't want to stop. Because if I stop…

KEN stops. Lights up on XI. XI reads a letter.

XI: **Dear Ken, I was pleased to hear that you are doing a sponsored run for us. I have just returned from the Zhangzhuang mine where 181 miners drowned after being trapped by flash floods last week. The people there are still in shock. They are angry that their story was given so little coverage in the news. I met a girl who goes to the mine every day and sits waiting for her brother to come out. We try to give the families all the help we can. I have set up a study to examine the causes of the flood and explore practical solutions with the authorities here. I wish you well. I have enclosed something for you. I will be there to meet you when you get to Beijing. Good luck. Xi.**

XI exits.

KEN: And so I run. Beside this raked earth, the colour of dried blood, this razor wire, these redoubts of sandbags and stone, past these soldiers' and armoured personnel carriers. Along the Turkish-Iraqi border…

SCENE 4

August 2007. A roadside in Turkey. Night. Moonlight.
KEN, JAHID, DINA, WEI. JAHID concludes telling WEI a joke.

JAHID: 'Oh, you don't want to worry about that,' says the barman, 'it's the peanuts – they're complimentary.'

WEI doesn't get the joke.

'Complimentary.' It means they're free. And it means paying someone a compliment. The peanuts are complimentary...

WEI: Com-pli-men-

DINA: It's not worth it, Wei. It's a terrible joke.

JAHID: That's the point. That's the basis of my act. It's post-modern. The jokes aren't really funny, but because they're not funny they are funny.

DINA: To you, maybe.

JAHID takes out a camera and starts filming DINA.

Put that thing away.

JAHID: It's for the blog.

DINA: Put it away. That's the Iraqi border over there. Jahid, they'll think we're Kurdish separatists and we'll all get – Jahid! Stop it!

JAHID stops filming.

JAHID: It's not like London here is it?

KEN: That's because it's Turkey.

DINA: Kurdistan.

JAHID: I bet it's still raining in London. All those poor sods hunched up outside the pubs, smoking their B&H getting soaked and freezing their nuts off.

WEI: (*Doesn't understand.*) Peanuts?

JAHID: (*Didn't hear him correctly.*) Penis?

KEN: (*Trying to explain.*) Testicles.

WEI: Their testicles will freeze off?

DINA: What a fascinating conversation.

KEN: It's just a figure of speech.

DINA: We need to decide who's sleeping in the car and who's sleeping out / here –

JAHID: I'm not sleeping outside.

DINA: Whatever happened to chivalry?

JAHID: Whatever happened to feminism? Besides I slept outside last night.

KEN: I'll sleep out.

DINA: You should sleep in the car. You need / a good rest…

KEN: No, really…really. I want to.

JAHID: He's going to sneak off to the nearest library.

WEI: **I will sleep here.**

KEN: You sure?

WEI nods.

Me and Wei will sleep out tonight.

JAHID: Great. (*Mocking the Olympic slogan.*) One World, One Dream!

DINA: Shut up.

JAHID exits.

I'll get the sleeping bags.

DINA exits.

KEN: We're doing well. So far… All right? You okay?

WEI nods.

Tomorrow. Long day.

WEI nods.

It must be…working for your dad, **Big Uncle,** it must be… I don't know. **Is that what you want?**

WEI: **Yes.**

DINA enters with sleeping bags.

KEN: **And you enjoy the work?**

WEI: **Yes.**

DINA: What was that?

KEN: I was just asking Wei about working for his Dad.

DINA: What do they do exactly?

WEI: (*To KEN.*) **What do we do?**

KEN nods.

We… (*To KEN.*) **I cannot… Will you translate?**

KEN: Sure. (*To DINA.*) I'll translate.

WEI: **We have developed 800,000 hectares of forest in Congo-Brazzaville.**

KEN: They've developed 800,000 somethings of forest. A lot of forest.

WEI: **Three out of every five trees on our land belongs to China. In the next twelve months we hope to double production to over one thousand trunks per day.**

KEN: Three out of every five trees on their land belongs to China. In the next year they're going to double production to over one thousand trunks per day.

DINA: That's sick.

KEN: Dina –

DINA: No. What do they think they're doing?

WEI: **We employ 600 Congolese who wouldn't have jobs.**

KEN: They employ 600 Congolese.

DINA: So the Communists think exploitation is fine now?

WEI looks to KEN for the translation of 'exploitation'.

KEN: **Exploitation.**

WEI: **Exploitation? No! We treat the Africans as equals. You still treat them as former subjects, as a charity case, instead of hand-outs we give them work. You don't know what you're talking about.**

KEN doesn't translate.

DINA: What? What did he say?

KEN: They treat Africans as equals not former subjects or charity cases.

DINA: Rubbish. What else? He said something else…

KEN: He said you don't know what you're talking about.

DINA: Tell him he's an idiot.

DINA turns her back and exits.

KEN: She gets a bit… You'd never know she was doing an MA in Peace and Reconciliation Studies.

WEI: **What?**

KEN: Nothing.

They get into their sleeping bags.

WEI: **Dina and Jahid, they were a couple?**

KEN: Dina and Jahid? Yes. No. Sort of. Jahid and Dina have been friends for years. But Jahid is gay.

WEI: **He is gay?**

KEN: His family are very religious. They're Muslim. Sunni. He's never told them. They were always going on at him about getting married so to shut them up he got Dina to pretend to be his girlfriend. But it only made matters worse. They didn't like Jahid seeing someone who wasn't Sunni. Dina's Dad was Shia and they didn't like that. When Jahid's Dad questioned Dina about her beliefs she told him she thought all religion was hocus-pocus and well…it was downhill from there. Can you understand?

WEI: I think.

KEN: Uncle must be proud of you.

WEI: **Proud?**

KEN: **Proud.** Yes.

WEI: Yes. Maybe.

KEN: I think I've always been a bit of a disappointment to my Dad. He wanted me to study medicine or law. Something sensible.

WEI: He is proud now.

KEN: Now? No, now he thinks I've gone completely nuts.

WEI: Peanuts?

KEN: Don't start that again. No – mad, insane…

WEI: No. You are not peanuts.

KEN: Thank you.

They are in their sleeping bags by now, looking up at the stars.

WEI: **Is Xi happy that you're doing this?**

KEN: Is Xi happy I'm doing this?

WEI: Yes.

KEN: I don't know. I think so. She sent me…

KEN shows WEI a jade pendent.

WEI: **Jade.** Jade. **It's beautiful.**

KEN: Yes. (*Lies back.*) You never see stars like this in London. Why's that do you think? Maybe I've just never looked. It's beautiful. Makes you feel…really small…

Silence as KEN and WEI drift off to sleep. Lights dim.

(*Voiceover.*) The land of Giantswallow lies in the northeast corner…

Lights up on XI.

XI: **In Sichuan province seventeen people were killed after the heavy rain triggered a mudslide.**

KEN: (*Voiceover.*) In the Thunder Swamp lives the Thunder God, he has the body of a dragon and the head of a man…

Lights up on a man wearing a suit that looks like it is made from the skin of a reptile[1] – this is LEI SHEN, Thunder God.

XI: **In Yunnan fourteen people died and many more are still missing as storms raged through the city of Zhaotong.**

KEN: (*Voiceover.*) When he drums on his belly…

---

1 Lei Shen, the Thunder god. He drums on his body to create thunder. His attribute is a dragon's body denoting rain. He was greatly feared and there are many remedies in the *Shan Hai Jing* for curing this phobia.

XI: **Over 600 people have now been killed by floods across China since the heavy rain began in June.**

There is a flash of lightning. LEI SHEN drums on his belly – as he does so we hear loud thunder. KEN sits up; frightened. He turns a torch on. XI and LEI SHEN have vanished. Silence – just the sound of KEN's heavy breathing.

WEI: Ken?

KEN: It's all right. I'm…It's fine. The thunder. Sorry…

KEN lies back down. He switches the torch off.

SCENE 5

August 2007. On one side of the stage is a portrait of Atatürk. On the other side of the stage is a portrait of the Ayatollah Khomeini. KEN, JAHID, DINA and WEI enter and stand before the portrait of Atatürk. JAHID is filming. DINA motions for him to put the camera away. He does. They face an (unseen) interrogator. The interrogator's questions are unheard.

Question: Why did you come this way?

KEN: It's the most direct route.

Question: You are aware that it is dangerous?

DINA: We knew it might be dangerous.

KEN: We checked with the Foreign Office.

JAHID: We're not going through Afghanistan.

DINA: And we haven't been in Iraq.

Question: Why are you doing this run?

KEN: It's for charity.

DINA: For victims of natural disasters.

JAHID: Global warming

Question: (To WEI.) Where are you from?

WEI: I'm from Beijing.

Question: What is your role in this activity?

WEI: I am translator. I speak Russian and Mandarin and a little English.

Question: (To DINA.) You are Iranian?

DINA: My father was Iranian. I'm a British Citizen.

Question: Is your father in Iran?

DINA: No. He's dead.

> *The interrogator instructs DINA to cover her hair. She pulls a scarf up onto her head, but leaves some hair showing.*

Sorry.

> *KEN, DINA, WEI and JAHID cross to the portrait of the Ayatollah Khomeini. Once again they face an (unseen) interrogator. The interrogator's questions are unheard.*

Question: What is the purpose of your visit?

KEN: It's a sponsored run.

JAHID: For charity.

DINA: For victims of the floods. In China.

KEN: And the drought.

JAHID: Global warming.

Question: What do you do?

WEI: I am translator.

Question: You intend to run to Beijing?

KEN: To Beijing, yes.

Statement: Good luck.

KEN: Thank you.

> *They get up to go. DINA is instructed to wait.*

DINA: Oh…

DINA waits. KEN, JAHID and WEI exit.
The interrogator asks DINA a question: Your father was Iranian?

DINA: Yes. He was from Tehran.

Question: Do you speak Farsi?

DINA: Yes, I speak…(*In Farsi.*) Yes, I speak some Farsi.

Question: Are you going to Tehran?

DINA: (*In Farsi.*) We're planning on stopping there, yes.

Question: You have family there?

DINA: (*In Farsi.*) My father's half-sister lives in Tehran.

Question: Your father is deceased?

DINA: (*In Farsi.*) Yes. He died in 1986.

Question: When did he leave Iran?

DINA: (*In Farsi.*) He left in…1983…no, 82, I think.

Question: Do you know why he left?

DINA: (*In Farsi.*) No. I don't know. I never… He… I was only two when he died.

Question: How did he die?

DINA: (*In Farsi.*) A car accident.

Question: Did he talk about the Iran-Iraq war?

DINA: (*In Farsi.*) The Iran-Iraq war? No. He never talked to me about it. Like I said, I was only two –

Question: Do you consider yourself to be British?

DINA: (*In Farsi.*) I am British. (*In English.*) Yes, British.

Question: Do you approve of American and British foreign policy in the Middle East?

DINA: (*In Farsi.*) Foreign policy?

Question: Do you think what America is doing is right?

DINA: (*In Farsi.*) I'm not American.

Question: But do you think this is right?

DINA: (*In Farsi.*) No. I don't think it's right.

Question: Your father did not fight for his country during the Iran-Iraq war?

DINA: (*In Farsi.*) My father couldn't fight in the Iran-Iraq war, he was in London.

Question: Perhaps he was a coward?

DINA: My father was not a coward.

> *The interrogator instructs DINA to completely cover her hair.*
> *She pulls the scarf to completely cover her hair.*
> *The interrogator tells her she can go. DINA exits.*

SCENE 6

September 2007. A room in a hotel in Tehran, Iran. JAHID is asleep in a large double bed. WEI is sitting on a sleeping bag on the floor next to the bed. KEN is sitting on the edge of the bed reading.
DINA is talking into her mobile phone.

DINA: (*On mobile – in Farsi.*) We're only here for one day… First thing?… About eight. Fine… Where is that?… No, I've got a map… I look forward to meeting you… Yes. Goodbye. (*Ends call.*) Wow.

KEN: Yes?

DINA: Yes. Tomorrow. I have to go to Doulat. Have you got the street map of Tehran?

> *KEN picks up a street map and passes it to her.*

KEN: You've never met her before?

DINA: Never. There are photographs of her and my Dad when they were kids. She's about ten years younger than him.

KEN: How well did you know your Dad?

DINA: Not at all really.

WEI: **She does not remember her father?**

KEN: No.

DINA: What was that?

KEN: Wei was asking if you remember your father.

DINA: I think I remember him…things that happened, but if I'm honest I probably invented them.

KEN: Like what?

DINA: Being carried to bed. Sitting on the draining board and being washed in the sink.

WEI: **Why did he leave Iran?**

KEN: Why did he leave Iran?

DINA: He didn't want to fight in the Iran-Iraq war.

WEI: **He refused to fight?**

DINA: What?

KEN: He wants to know if your Dad refused to fight.

DINA: (*To WEI.*) Yes. He did.

WEI: What he… **What work did he do?**

KEN: What was his job?

DINA: He was unemployed.

WEI: It is bad not to work.

DINA: He couldn't get a job. At least my Father didn't strip another country of its natural resources.

WEI: No –

DINA: That's what yours does, isn't it?

WEI: No! No! **We are bringing help and co-operation to Africa.**

DINA: What?

KEN: Look I really don't think / this is a…

DINA: What did he say!?!

KEN: They're helping Africa.

DINA: Like fuck they are!

KEN: **Like fuck –**

WEI: I understand! You wrong!

DINA: Shall we talk about China's human rights record?

KEN: No!

WEI: **What about Guantanamo?**

DINA: Tibet?

WEI: **Northern Ireland?**

DINA: Tiananmen?

WEI: **Iraq?** Iraq?

DINA: I'm not responsible for my government does!

WEI: **I'm not responsible for what my country does!**

DINA: What?

KEN: He's not responsible for what his country does.

WEI: **What?**

KEN: **I was just –**

DINA: What?

KEN: Will you two please learn to argue in the same language!!!

JAHID sits up.

JAHID: Will you all just shut up! I thought this was supposed to be a 'Journey of Harmony'? 'One World, One Dream,' people! Remember?

DINA exits. WEI gets into his sleeping bag. Both of them disgruntled. KEN gets into bed beside JAHID.

No touching.

KEN: You're not my type.

KEN reads his book.

JAHID: (*Pointing to an illustration in KEN's book.*) What's that?

KEN: The nine-tailed fox.

JAHID: Why's it got nine tails?

KEN: Because it has.

JAHID: What does it mean?

KEN: (*Reads from the book.*) 'Mount Base…there is an animal here, shaped like a fox, but with nine tails; it makes the sound of a baby. Whoever eats it will be immune to malicious forces.'

JAHID: Better eat some then. (*Pointing to another picture.*) What's that supposed to be?

KEN: A horse.

JAHID: It's got stripes.

KEN: Like a tiger, yes.

JAHID: And a white head.

KEN: Yes.

JAHID: And a red tail.

KEN: And if you wear its fur around your waist, it will help you to produce many children. Xi used to love this drawing. She said we should get it framed and tell the story to our children.

KEN flicks through the book.

Here's one for you… (*Reading.*) 'There is a kind of plant…' blah, blah… '…yellow flower and red fruit called the wild strawberry. If you eat it, you will become beautiful and sexy.'

JAHID: I'll remember that.

KEN sighs; sniffs.

You all right?

KEN: Yes.

JAHID feels KEN's forehead.

JAHID: You've got a temperature.

KEN: I'm fine. Let's get some sleep.

KEN turns the light out. After a moment, we hear the sound of a baby crying. In the darkness…

Can anyone hear that?

WEI: It's a baby.

A moment of silence. The sound of a baby crying again.
KEN turns the light back on. Sitting at the foot of the bed is XI – she is stroking a fox with nine tails. Only KEN sees this.
JAHID turns the light off again.
KEN puts it back on. XI and the fox have gone.

JAHID: What's the problem?

KEN: I want to leave the light on. Just for a while.

JAHID: Tough!

JAHID turns the light off.

SCENE 7

October 2007. Iran. On the road to Mashad. KEN is sitting on a roadside clutching his leg. An IRANIAN WOMAN in a chador is standing over him. (Note: played by performer playing DINA.)
An Iranian MAN in a long coat with his hands in his pockets[1] stands watching them. The IRANIAN WOMAN speaks Farsi.

IRANIAN WOMAN: Do you want me to get help?

KEN: I don't understand.

IRANIAN WOMAN: I can get a doctor.

KEN: I've pulled a hamstring.

IRANIAN WOMAN: Do you want me to get a doctor?

KEN: Doc…? I don't understand.

IRANIAN WOMAN: There's a hospital not far from here in Mashad. Have you got a pen? I can draw you a map.

KEN: Do you know what day it is today?

IRANIAN WOMAN: What?

KEN: 16th October. I was supposed to be getting married today.

IRANIAN WOMAN: I don't speak English. I can try to find someone…?

JAHID enters.

JAHID: What happened?

KEN: My hamstring.

IRANIAN WOMAN: Is there anything I can do?

JAHID: Sorry, I don't understand.

IRANIAN WOMAN: Do you have pen and paper?

---

1 When this man appears holding yellow snakes in his hands and with yellow snakes emerging from his mouth and ears there will be a flood.

JAHID: What?

IRANIAN WOMAN: I'll be back in a minute.

The IRANIAN WOMAN exits.

JAHID: What did she want?

KEN: I don't know.

JAHID: Can you put any weight on it?

KEN tries to stand, he winces in pain and sits back down. DINA and WEI enter. DINA wears a scarf on her head. Her arms are bare.

DINA: Is it bad?

KEN: I'll be fine.

WEI and JAHID help KEN to his feet.
KEN puts some weight on his leg – it's painful.

DINA: You'll have to stop / for today…

KEN: I can't stop.

DINA: Don't be stupid.

DINA feels KEN's forehead.

You're burning up. You shouldn't be running at all.

KEN: There's nothing / wrong with me…

DINA: You're not well.

KEN: I'm –

DINA: You're sick, Ken.

JAHID: What are we going to do?

WEI: **I can run in his place.**

KEN: No.

DINA: What?

WEI: **Let me run.**

DINA: Wei?

WEI: I run.

KEN: No. The whole point of this is that I'm doing it solo. That's why people have sponsored me… It's about endurance.

DINA: (*To KEN.*) You can't run.

JAHID: We could drive –

KEN: No. Absolutely not.

JAHID: Who's going to know?

KEN: I am.

WEI: I run.

KEN: No. No way.

The IRANIAN WOMAN re-enters. (Note: now played by performer playing XI.) She takes out a piece of paper. She holds it out for KEN.

KEN: What?

DINA: (*To the IRANIAN WOMAN – in Farsi.*) Can I see?

The IRANIAN WOMAN hands the piece of paper to DINA.

It's directions. There's a hospital not too far from here on the road to Mashad. (*In Farsi.*) Hospital?

The IRANIAN WOMAN nods.

KEN: I don't need a hospital.

DINA: Yes you do. (*In Farsi.*) Thank you.

MAN IN COAT: (*In Farsi.*) Whore! (*Jen-de!*)

DINA: (*In Farsi.*) What did you call me?

JAHID: Dina?

> *The IRANIAN WOMAN whispers something in DINA's ear (she is telling DINA to cover her arms). The IRANIAN WOMAN exits.*

What was that –

DINA: Nothing.

KEN: I'm not going to a hospital.

DINA: You have to get it checked. What if you run on it and make it worse?

JAHID: We'll need somewhere to stay tonight.

WEI: I find somewhere.

DINA: I'll drive the car up.

> *DINA and WEI exit. KEN turns away from JAHID. He catches the eye of the MAN IN THE LONG COAT with his hands in his pockets. The man takes his hands from his pockets; he is holding yellow snakes in his fists. Yellow snakes crawl from his mouth and his ears. KEN collapses.*

JAHID: Ken!

SCENE 8

October 2007. Car. Iranian music. DINA drives. JAHID sits in the front passenger seat eating strawberries. They are in heavy traffic. KEN is sitting in the back, intermittently dozing and looking out of the window. They pass the man we saw earlier wearing a suit that looks like it is made from the skin of a reptile (LEI SHEN, the god of Thunder). He drums on his belly – as he does so we hear thunder.

JAHID: That was really close.

> *The thunder continues intermittently during the following section.*

What did that man say to you?

DINA: He called me a whore.

JAHID: I told you to cover up.

DINA: I never knew my bare arms could have that Effect on a man.

JAHID: You've got sexy elbows.

DINA: Sexy elbows?

JAHID: Yes.

DINA: Can elbows be sexy?

JAHID: Yes. I hope Wei finds somewhere decent to stay.

JAHID eats another strawberry.

DINA: Are you going to eat all of those strawberries?

JAHID: Yes.

DINA: You'll be sick.

JAHID: I'll be gorgeous.

DINA: What are you talking about?

JAHID: Nothing. (*Referring to the posters of the martyrs.*) I thought we'd seen the last of these posters in Tehran.

DINA: My aunt told me six of our family died in the Iran-Iraq war. She's an amazing woman. She said over one million Iranians were killed or wounded.

JAHID: That many?

DINA: And guess who financed Saddam Hussein? The Americans.

A shoal of flying fish with birds' wings swim passed the car. Only KEN seems to notice.

KEN: (*Voiceover.*) The River Meng flows south into the River Yang. There are flying fish here which sound like mandarin ducks. Wherever they appear…

There is a blinding flash of lightning; a loud peel of thunder. XI appears next to the car.

XI: **In Guangxi, heavy rain has destroyed 610 homes, 29 reservoirs, 362 embankments, 165 roads and forced 59 factories to close…**

The sky grows dark.
It starts to pour with rain – a deluge.

JAHID: Here it comes.

XI: **When the Yangtze flooded on June 23, the floodwaters flushed out millions of rats, which have spread out and ravaged farmland.**

JAHID: Have you heard from Xi? Is she still in China?

DINA: She's in Sichuan. She said the place she's staying has been devastated. It's just mud. People's houses were washed away. There's no power, no sanitation.

JAHID: Do you really think it's global warming?

DINA: I think climate change has got something to do with it, yes. Why?

JAHID: Should we be driving?

DINA: You have to see the bigger picture, J. Xi said the blog is attracting lots of interest. We're doing a good thing. She's threatening to take us all to an opera when we get to Beijing to celebrate.

JAHID: Chinese opera?

DINA: Yes.

JAHID: Scary.

DINA: You never know. You might like it. (*Beat.*) Is he still hot?

JAHID feels KEN's forehead.

JAHID: Yes.

DINA: I hope he's going to be all right. God, this rain is incredible.

Horns sound – the car grinds to a halt.
They are in a traffic jam.

Shit.

JAHID: The traffic's solid.

DINA: The hospital can't be much further. Why don't you check?

JAHID: I'm not getting out in this.

DINA: Jahid!

JAHID: Fine! Fine!

JAHID gets out of the car and runs off.
DINA turns to KEN.

DINA: Ken?

KEN is semi-conscious. She feels his forehead.
She is concerned. She looks to see how far JAHID has gone.

DINA: Not that way! Jahid! Shit! I'll be back in a minute.

DINA gets out of the car and exits. Lightning. LEI SHEN drums on his belly. A violent clap of thunder. Music. LEI SHEN orchestrates the storm. There is more lightning. More thunder. Torrential rain.

LEI SHEN: (*Lyric.*) **Lightning flash**
Thunder roll
Rocks roar
Crows caw
Wind thrash
Rain lash
Trees groan
Seeds unsown
Mud slide
Beasts drown
Swollen tide
Ships down
Banks burst
Humans cursed.

(*Spoken.*) **I am Lei Shen, Thunder God.**

> **I will not be controlled**
> **Louder than nine volcanoes**
> **My violence behold**
> **Now you hear me**
> **Now you don't.**

XI steps out of the car. The stage starts to flood. The waters are rising. XI is swept away by the flood.

KEN: Xi!

XI: **Help...**

KEN: Xi!!!

XI: **Help me...**

KEN: Xi!!!

XI: **I love...**

KEN gets out of the car and attempts to make his way to where he last saw XI, but the waters engulf him. He re-emerges and tries to swim against the current, but it is hopeless and he once again disappears beneath the waters and sinks to the ground where he lies motionless on his back. As KEN lies underwater his belly starts to distend. A moment later, the demigod, YÜ,[1] is born by parthenogenesis from KEN's belly. YÜ floats to the surface and scrambles up onto a mound above the flood.

YÜ: (*Lyric.*) **I am Yü, son of Kun**
> **Queller of the world flood**
> **Lightning flash**
> **Thunder roll**
> **Raging flood**
> **I will control**
> **Wind thrash**
> **Mud slide**
> **From destiny**

---

1 Yü, a demigod, queller of the world flood.

> I will not hide
> Rain lash
> River swell
> These floodwaters
> I will quell
> I am Yü, son of Kun
> Queller of the world flood
> Saviour of the drowned world.

LEI SHEN squares up to YÜ.

LEI SHEN: (*Lyric.*) **I am Lei Shen, Thunder God
  I will not be controlled!**

LEI SHEN orchestrates the storm, whipping up a whirlwind. The flood increases. YÜ tries to stop LEI SHEN, but LEI SHEN is incredibly strong and pushes YÜ away. LEI SHEN is angry; he turns the storm into a typhoon. YÜ grabs him again and they fight as the typhoon lashes around them. LEI SHEN lunges with his fists; he leaps about in a frenzy, the typhoon intensifying all the time. Eventually, LEI SHEN knocks YÜ into the waters.

LEI SHEN: (*Lyric.*) **I am Lei Shen, Thunder God
  I will not be controlled!**

*LEI SHEN exits. The storm subsides a little.
YÜ emerges from beneath the waters and pulls himself up onto a promontory to survey the devastation around him.*

YÜ: (*Spoken.*) **Workers, come. There is much to do if we are to save this drowned world.**

Workers enter and he directs them to build dams and channels for the floodwater. They work hard.

(*Lyric.*) **I am Yü
  Builder of dams
  I am Yü
  Channeller of rivers
  Night and day we will toil
  Week after week
  Year after year**

> **I am Yü, queller of the world flood.**

At last the work is nearing completion. But just as it appears that the flood will finally be controlled, LEI SHEN re-enters.

LEI SHEN: (*Lyric.*) **I am Lei Shen, Thunder God**
> **I will not be controlled!**

LEI SHEN destroys the dam.

> **Lightning flash**
> **Thunder roll!**

LEI SHEN beats on his belly. Loud thunder sounds as he orchestrates another storm. It is terrifying in its intensity.

YÜ: (*Lyric.*) **I am Yü, queller of the world flood**
> **Now you will be controlled!**

YÜ and LEI SHEN once again do battle. YÜ grabs LEI SHEN's tail and pulls. As he pulls, LEI SHEN's tail starts to extend. It stretches longer and longer until it is several metres in length. LEI SHEN is pulled off stage. The god is beaten, the storm subsides, but all of YÜ's hard work has been undone by the storm and the world is flooded again.

> (*Spoken.*) **Our work lies in ruins. Now it seems the flood will claim us.**

XI re-enters, in the guise of NÜ CH'OU chih shih[1] wearing a green dress.

NÜ CHOU: (*Lyric.*) **I am Nü Ch'ou chih shih**
> **Goddess**
> **Second of the Twelve Earth branches**
> **I bring regeneration**

---

1 Nü Ch'ou chih shih, a goddess belonging to solar myth. She was exposed on a mountain to the heat of the ten suns which all appeared in the sky at once. She died, but was resurrected as a goddess. Her gesture of screening her face with her green sleeve is a ritual pose to ward off the heat of the ten suns or hide her disfigured face. The colour of her sleeve denotes the regeneration of life on earth following the solar disaster, when the world is saved and reborn. She is often depicted holding a crab, a symbol of regeneration.

I bring rebirth
I wear green for new life
I wear green for new earth
I am life reborn, like the phoenix
Life anew.

YÜ crosses to NÜ CH'OU. He bows to her.

(*Spoken.*) **You have defeated Lei Shen.**

YÜ: (*Spoken.*) **Yes, but the dams we built have burst open; the channels we dug are blocked. The river destroys all in its path. Please, Nü Ch'ou, we have so little time. The people are starving; they are dying from disease and malnutrition; the high ground is overcrowded, wars are being fought in the tree tops...**

NÜ CHOU: (*Spoken.*) **Dam the floodwaters at their deepest point. Sluice off the Great River. Cleave open the mountain of dragon pass and call it Dragon Gate. Dig new channels; build new earthworks...**

YÜ: (*Spoken.*) **But there is no time...**

NÜ CHOU: (*Lyric.*) **Yellow Dragon, Yellow Dragon**
　　Drag your tail
　　Create a channel.

A Yellow Dragon enters, dragging its long tail behind it, creating a channel for the water.

　　(*Lyric.*) **Yellow Dragon, Yellow Dragon**
　　Build earthworks
　　Disperse these waters.

The Yellow Dragon carries mud on its back to create earthworks against the floodwaters. Finally the flood is quelled.
YÜ turns to NÜ CH'OU.

YÜ: (*Spoken.*) **Nü Ch'ou, thank you, the work is done.**

YÜ bows to NÜ CH'OU. NÜ CH'OU exits. The workers cheer and raise YÜ up onto their shoulders.

WORKER: (*Spoken.*) **All praise Yü the Great! If it had not been for Yü, we would have all been fishes!**

The workers carry YÜ off. KEN re-appears, tries to stand and falls.

KEN: Xi? Xi!!!

DINA re-enters.

DINA: Ken! What are you doing out here! You're soaked!

KEN: Was that Xi?

DINA: What? Come on. Let's get you back in the car.

DINA helps KEN to his feet.

SCENE 9

December 2007. Iran. Mashad. Hotel room.

KEN: I want to go tomorrow.

DINA: Are you sure?

KEN: Just a few miles. I'll be all right. I want to get to Turkmenistan. It's Christmas in a couple of weeks.

DINA: I know. I know.

KEN: I'll have to run a full marathon every day.

DINA: Fine. Get injured again.

KEN: I know what I'm doing.

KEN exits into bathroom.

JAHID: We've lost a lot of time.

DINA: I know.

JAHID: The website's had hundreds of hits. There are loads of donations coming in.

DINA: That's good isn't it?

JAHID: I've been telling everybody it's going great in the blog. They haven't got a clue we're stuck here. They think we're halfway across Turkmenistan.

DINA: Tell them the truth, then.

JAHID: What?

DINA: Tell them Ken's injured. We're behind schedule. We've got problems. It's a struggle. People like to hear that kind of stuff. We'll probably get more sponsors if people know we're up against it.

*WEI enters from hallway,
KEN enters from bathroom.*

KEN: Are the visas sorted?

DINA: Yes. Stop worrying.

WEI: **There is something I have to tell you. Privately.**

KEN: Yes?

WEI: **I have run out of money.**

KEN: But I thought…?

DINA: What?

KEN: Wei said he's run out of money.

WEI: **I said it was private.**

KEN: Not when it affects everybody else.

DINA: Run out? I thought he was loaded?

KEN: (*To WEI.*) **Are you serious?**

WEI: **I have no money left.**

KEN: **I don't understand.**

WEI: **No money!**

DINA: Ken?

KEN: He says he's got nothing left.

DINA: (*To WEI.*) How come? Why? What happened?

KEN: **What happened?**

WEI: **I can't tell you.**

KEN: **Why?**

WEI: **I can't!**

DINA: Was he robbed? Say something…

WEI: **No! No I can't! You don't understand!**

KEN: What's going on? Wei? We're family. **Tell us. Please…**

WEI: **I'm no good. My Father sent me away. He told me to sort my life out. I decided to learn English so that I could move to London or America.**

KEN: **Why?**

WEI: **I lost a lot of money. In casinos. Gambling. My Father was very angry. He gave me enough money for a year. He told me to come back when I had stopped gambling. It's all gone. The money he gave me. I lost what was left last night playing cards.** (*In English.*) Sorry.

WEI exits.

DINA: What was that?

KEN: His Dad sent him away to stop him gambling. It had nothing to do with work. He had enough money for a year, to sort himself out. But he's lost what was left. Gambling last night.

DINA: What are we going to do?

KEN: I'll try and get a loan. I was going to do anyway before Wei stepped in to cover our costs. I don't want to use sponsorship money.

DINA: I've got some money with me. Jahid – what about you?

JAHID: Yes.

DINA: My money should be enough to pay for the hotel.

KEN: Thanks. Look, I'd better see if he's all right.

KEN exits.

SCENE 10

January 2008. Running sequence. Turkmenistan. Music. Darkness – night. KEN running, illuminated by the green flame of the torch. Carousel of a disembodied horse.[1]

KEN: I'm running. In this green light. In this cold. Past this frozen desert. Through this brittle night air. Past this blue lunar landscape. Through this snow in the Karakum desert. Past these strange shapes. Past something that looks like a giant. Past something that looks like a…

We hear something that sounds like a howling dog.
KEN stops running.

(*Voiceover.*) Five hundred leagues further south is Mount Anvil. There is an animal here, shaped like a horse, with ram's eyes, four horns, and an ox's tail. Its name is You-you. Wherever it appears, the country will have deceitful strangers…

KEN runs.

---

1 The far-far horse has the eyes of a ram, four horns, and an ox's tail.

SCENE 11

March 2008. Roadside. Uzbekistan. Bukhara.
A rundown garage exterior. The car has broken down.

KEN: What are we going to do if they can't get it started?

JAHID: Pray.

KEN: I don't believe in God.

JAHID: You could start.

KEN: I'm going to / see what they're…

JAHID: Wait! Ken, wait… Dina will sort it out.

KEN: I should be running.

JAHID: And what happens if you get halfway to Samarkand and we're still stuck here trying to get the car fixed?

KEN: This is hopeless! We should be in Kyrgyzstan by now, not stuck / in some…

JAHID: Stop panicking.

KEN: I want to panic! I feel like panicking!

JAHID: Think about something else.

KEN: Like what?

JAHID: Like personal hygiene.

KEN: What?

JAHID: You smell.

KEN: I smell? You smell!

JAHID: I know I smell. You smell worse than me.

KEN: I do not.

A long haired cat[1] enters and sits watching them.
KEN stares at it for a moment then turns back to JAHID.

Can you see that cat?

JAHID: (*Answering KEN's question.*) Yes.

KEN: You're sure you can see it?

JAHID: Yes.

KEN: I'm not imagining it?

JAHID: No. Here puss…

JAHID takes out his camera and starts to film the cat.
DINA and WEI enter.

KEN: Well?

WEI: **No good.**

DINA: It's had it. Scrap. They want to break it up for parts.

KEN: Shit.

DINA: They offered to sell us a truck. A Soviet…something…

WEI: Gaz.

DINA: It's ancient.

KEN: How old?

DINA: 1970s I think.

JAHID: We haven't got any money.

KEN: We'll have to use sponsorship money. We can pay it back. How much do they want for it?

DINA: We wanted to talk to you first.

KEN: Can we see it?

---

1 An hermaphroditic wild cat with long fur – if you see this cat you should eat some of it so that you don't become jealous (or maybe it's just a cat?)

DINA: Yes. Ken, there's something else, though, before we…

KEN: What?

DINA: They let me use their telephone in the garage to ring the charity.

KEN: Did you tell them we're behind schedule?

DINA: Yes –

KEN: Are they concerned we might miss the opening ceremony?

DINA: Yes. But that's not… I spoke to Xi. She's leaving China. She's got a job with an NGO in Washington advising on drought relief programmes.

KEN: Washington? Is she still going to meet us in Beijing?

DINA: She doesn't think she'll be able to make it.

KEN: She said she would be there to meet me… She told me she would be going back to her job in London. Does she have any intention of moving back to the UK?

DINA: I don't know. I don't think so.

KEN turns away. He is devastated.

Ken, I'm sorry.

KEN is crying.

KEN: What am I supposed to do? I've just… I've just run all this way. What am I trying to prove?

JAHID: Ken –

KEN: No. I've had it. That's it. Finished.

JAHID: You can't just give up.

KEN: No?

JAHID: What about raising money / for the charity –

KEN: Screw the money! Screw the charity!

JAHID: Ken. Come on. I thought you wanted to do something? I thought you wanted to show you cared. Isn't that what this is about? This isn't a theory; it's happening. You're doing it. You're not sitting in the library trying to write the longest footnote in the history of longest footnotes, you're half way to China on a sponsored run. This isn't boring. Aggravating. Annoying. Dirty. Filthy. Smelly. Yes! But not boring. We don't know what's going to happen from one day to the next. We can't control things. You can't control things. Ken, listen to me, Ken… You are no longer suffering from obsessive-compulsive disorder. You have been cured. I'm being serious! You've got to see this through or you're going to hate yourself. In six months time… Ken, come on. Look… Look where we are. It's insane. It's brilliant. Look how far we've come. I've seen places I never even knew existed. I've eaten things I can't even pronounce the name of. We're standing outside a garage in Bukhara, in Uzbekistan. How mad is that? I'd usually be at *Phones 4 U* on Oxford Street at this time of day thinking about whether I can be arsed to go to Sainsbury's or not on my way home from work. This is… I don't know. Something! Don't give up now, Ken. We've come too far…

Pause.

DINA: Ken…if you need some time to think / about all this…

KEN: No. No. Jahid's right. People have sponsored me. This isn't about me and my ex. This is about…more… I don't know. Where's this truck?

DINA: Are you sure?

WEI: **You want to continue?**

KEN: Yes. I want to continue.

JAHID: Good man.

DINA: What about Beijing? We'll never make up the time.

KEN: Yes we will.

DINA: How?

KEN: We'll drive. We'll drive through Tajikistan and Kyrgyzstan then we'll pick up the run again once we get across the border into China.

WEI: **Drive to China?**

KEN: Yes. We'll drive to Kashgar. I want to carry on. Even if I do end up like Hsing T'ien.

DINA: Like who?

KEN: Never mind. Come on. Where's this truck?

WEI leads the way, the others follow.

SCENE 12

April 2008. Driving sequence. Tajikistan. WEI drives, DINA snoozes next to him in the passenger seat. JAHID and KEN sit in the open back of the truck. KEN stares out into the middle-distance. JAHID is reading a newspaper. It is hot.

KEN: (*Voiceover.*) The Country of One-Arm lies to the north... Hsing-Tien fought for the godhead here. His head was cut off, but he refused to yield. And so Hsing Tien became the example of the great failed hero...

JAHID shows KEN something in the newspaper.

JAHID: Look... Someone tried to grab the torch in London. There have been demos in Greece, London, Paris...mostly about Tibet.

KEN: How old is this?

JAHID: Couple of weeks. So much for the *Journey of Harmony*. They've had more problems than we have. And that's saying something.

The truck comes to a halt. WEI tries to restart the truck. It won't start.

KEN: What's wrong?

WEI: Too hot. **I think it's overheated.**

KEN: I'll take a look.

KEN goes to jump off the back of the truck, but then stops. We hear the sounds of 'Jiu-you, Jiu-you...' [1]

KEN turns back to JAHID.

Jahid!

JAHID: Yes?

They listen.

What?

KEN: Nothing.

In the distance we can hear a thrumming noise, it is growing steadily louder.

JAHID: What's that...? Can you hear that noise?

KEN listens.

What is it?

KEN: I don't know.

KEN jumps off the truck. He takes a couple of steps – the ground beneath his feet crunches. He stops; looks down.
JAHID jumps down, he takes a few steps, stops.

JAHID: What the.. ?

KEN: I think they're locusts.[2]

KEN stoops down to investigate.

---

1 Whenever this creature appears locusts will cause great damage in the area.
2 A woman farmer from Tajikistan, Umeda Ddinaeva, is quoted in an Oxfam report on the impact of climate change on poor people dependent on the land in Central Asia as saying: 'Locusts attacked our fields and our entire crop has disappeared. I have noticed that when the temperature is above 34 degrees, when it is much hotter than usual, there is more chance that locusts will come.'

They are. Look.

The sound is getting closer. KEN crunches round to the front of the truck and opens the bonnet. WEI and DINA get out.
They take a few steps; look down.

JAHID: Locusts.

KEN: (*Plucking a dead locust from the radiator.*) Shit… Look…

DINA: Locusts? This time of year?

KEN: (*To himself.*) That's what it was.

DINA: What?

KEN: A creature that cries 'Jiu-you, Jiu-you…'

DINA: What about it?

KEN: Whenever this creature appears locusts will cause great damage in that area.

DINA: What are you talking about?

KEN: Forget it.

KEN and JAHID start to remove locusts from the engine and radiator. The sound is getting closer. A man enters; he is spraying the ground with insecticide, he wears a protective mask/helmet.

(*To WEI.*) Can you ask him if there is anywhere we can get some water for the radiator?

WEI crosses to talk to the man. DINA helps KEN and JAHID to remove the locusts from the engine and radiator.

JAHID: You can eat locusts.

DINA: Don't be ridiculous.

JAHID: You can. They're good for you. Stir-fried, roasted, boiled.

DINA: That is such crap.

JAHID: It is not!

The noise is really close now. WEI re-joins them.

WEI: No water.

KEN: Great.

WEI: **He said locust swarms are on the increase in Tajikistan, even at this time of year.**

JAHID: What was that?

KEN: Locust swarms are on the increase in Tajikistan, even at this time of year.

KEN looks over at the man with the insecticide spray. The man pulls off his mask/helmet – he has no head.[1] KEN stares at him – only KEN sees this. The man replaces his mask/helmet and exits. The noise is even closer.

JAHID: (*Still pulling locusts form the engine.*) There are hundreds / of them…

Locusts swarm across the stage.

DINA: Shit! What the!?

WEI grabs DINA's hand. They all run off. A plague of locusts invade the stage.

SCENE 13

Later. The interior of a large, steel, freight container. The green flame of the Olympic torch throws strange shadows. KEN, JAHID, DINA and WEI are sitting with the TAJIK MAN – now with a head. He is sharing food with them. KEN, JAHID and WEI eat hungrily. DINA is uncertain.

DINA: What is it? What is…? No meat. Me. No meat.

TAJIK MAN: Plov.

---

1 Hsing T'ien, a demigod and failed warrior hero. He challenged a god for supremacy and lost. His struggle to continue the fight despite being decapitated won him admirers as the model of the courageous failed hero.

DINA: What?

TAJIK MAN: Plov. Shashlik.

JAHID: It's good.

DINA: What is it? God, I'm starving!

JAHID: Tastes like chicken.

DINA: (*To TAJIK MAN.*) Chicken? This – chicken?

DINA does a chicken impersonation. The TAJIK MAN joins in.

Oh sod it.

DINA eats. The TAJIK MAN takes out a bottle of vodka and pours shots for his new friends. They drink in the Russian manner – glasses drained with each toast.

TAJIK MAN: Saman Khuda![1]

They all cheer and down their drinks in one. The TAJIK MAN refills glasses.

Rudaki![2]

Repeat action.

Manchester United!

Repeat action.

JAHID: Butlins!

Repeat action.

Nigella Lawson!

Repeat action.

KEN: Jamie Oliver!

Repeat action.

---

1 Ancestor of the Samanids and a source of Tajik nationalism.
2 Persian poet important to culture of Tajikistan.

WEI: James Bond!

Repeat action.

DINA: Can we slow down a bit? (*Repeat action.*) No, I'm serious. (*Repeat action.*) Please…

JAHID: So there's this man and he's / having

DINA: Oh no…

JAHID: Listen… Listen… There's this man and he's having lunch in some sandwich place, when this gorgeous woman sits down next to him. And he's like…it must be my lucky day. But he hasn't got the nerve to talk to her, right. Then, suddenly she sneezes and her glass eye shoots out. He's got good reflexes this bloke and quick as a flash he sticks out a hand, catches it and gives it back her. 'Oh dear, I am so sorry,' the woman says popping her eye back in. 'Let me buy you a coffee.' They have a coffee, and afterwards, the woman's like 'Let's go out for a meal.' After paying for everything, she asks him if he wants to come back to her place and stay the night. And he's like, 'Yes…'

DINA: Dream on.

JAHID: The next morning, she cooks him a slap up breakfast with all the trimmings. The bloke's in ecstasy! 'You know,' he says, 'you are the perfect woman. Are you this nice to every bloke you meet?' 'No,' she says, 'you just happened to catch my eye.'

Groans. DINA tries to explain the joke to WEI. WEI tries to explain the joke to the TAJIK MAN. The TAJIK MAN grabs his insecticide container and starts to drum. DINA and WEI dance. JAHID and KEN join them. DINA and WEI collapse in a heap. They kiss. JAHID watches them for a moment; then KEN pulls him back into their dance.

One World! One Dream!

KEN: Shut up.

JAHID: These two aerials meet on a roof…

KEN: No…

JAHID: These two aerials meet on a roof…

KEN puts his hand over JAHID's mouth to stop him telling another joke. They wrestle. At first it's playful then it turns nasty.

DINA: Jahid! Ken! Stop it!

They wrestle. WEI and the TAJIK MAN finally succeed in pulling them apart. Only for them to break free and start wrestling again. JAHID pushes KEN away knocking the torch off and throwing the scene into total darkness. KEN turns the torch back on. DINA, WEI and JAHID are gone. KEN is standing face to face with a headless man – Hsing T'ien/Form Sky.[1] He is holding a battleaxe and a shield. He does a war dance. He lifts his axe above KEN's head and swings it down. The lights snap out. KEN screams. A moment later the torch comes back on. The TAJIK MAN and everyone else are back in their original positions. JAHID is standing over KEN. JAHID storms out.

What was all that about?

The TAJIK MAN offers KEN vodka.

KEN: No, no…I've had enough…Thanks.

JAHID re-enters. The others turn to look at him.

JAHID: Someone's nicked the truck.

SCENE 14

May 2008. Kyrgyzstan. KEN, JAHID, DINA and WEI are squashed onto a bus with (unseen) locals, chickens, traders and their goods. They have been travelling for a long time and are exhausted.

KEN: (*Voiceover.*) We're driving on this bus. In this heat. With these locals, these chickens, these Kyrgyz and Uighur traders and their goods, their radios, their pots and pans. In this smell of animals and perspiration. Through this gorge, between razor sharp rocks and dried up streams, towards the Chinese border…

---

[1] Hsing T'ien (see above, Scene 12).

DINA and WEI are in the middle of another argument.

WEI: **If you measure it in terms of bowls of rice, each person in China causes the equivalent of one rice bowl of pollution, compared to each person in the west who causes three rice bowls of pollution.**

KEN: In terms of bowls of rice, each person in China causes the one rice bowl of pollution, compared to each person in the West who causes three rice bowls of pollution.

DINA: What has rice got to do with it?

JAHID: I'm starving.

WEI: **China is building eco-cities, environmentally sustainable cities. Are you?**

KEN: China is building eco-cities, environmentally sustainable cities, are you?

DINA: China builds two new coal-fired power stations every week! (*To KEN.*) Translate.

KEN: No! I'm sick of this! Why can't you stop arguing? It's ridiculous.

JAHID: (*Joking.*) One World, One Dream!

KEN: Shut up!

The bus judders to a halt.

Now what?

WEI: Police.

JAHID: Not again…

They watch as an (unseen) police officer makes his way along the bus.

KEN: We don't have any drugs. No drugs.

WEI: **No drugs…** No drugs. (*In Russian.*) No drugs… (*Net narcotikov…*)

WEI listens as the officer says something to him.

We must get off.

KEN: No drugs.

WEI: (*In Russian.*) No drugs. (*Net narcotikov.*)

DINA: We better do as they say.

KEN, JAHID, DINA and WEI get off the bus. They unpack their belongings and leave them strewn on the ground for inspection. They wait for their things to be searched.
DINA wanders off to one side. JAHID joins her.

JAHID: So you and Wei…?

DINA: What about us?

JAHID: Is it… I don't know…serious.

DINA: Maybe…

JAHID makes his way back towards KEN.
KEN is staring up into the sky.
We hear a bird call 'Suan-yu, suan-yu'.

KEN: Three hundred leagues further south is a mountain called Mount Jing. On its north face bloodstone is abundant. There is a bird here…

JAHID: Ken?

KEN points up into the sky.
There doesn't seem to be anything there.

KEN: Suan-Yu. Wherever it appears, there will be panic.

Gunshots.

JAHID: Shit!

More gunshots. Panic. The people who boarded the bus aren't police, they are bandits. One of them is barking orders.

WEI: Empty pockets. Empty. Do as they say.

DINA: They're not police!

KEN: What's going on?

WEI: **Quickly!**

They empty their pockets. More barked orders.

Get down. On the ground. Face down. Quick.

KEN, JAHID, DINA and WEI lay face down on the ground. A mumble of voices and the sound of activity as the bandits steal from the passengers. More shots. DINA screams. The sound of a truck driving away. KEN, JAHID and WEI sit up. DINA is sobbing.

Dina?

WEI turns DINA over; one of the legs of her jeans is soaked in blood. WEI quickly fashions a tourniquet to stem the bleeding.
KEN inspects the wound.

JAHID: Is she…?

KEN: I think it passed straight through. Wei, let me… You find out where the nearest hospital is. You are the only one who speaks Russian. Go.

KEN takes over bandaging DINA's leg. WEI exits.

SCENE 14A

Airport departures. KEN and JAHID with DINA and WEI.
DINA holds a crutch.

FLIGHT ANNOUNCER: (*Voiceover.*) **Hainan Airlines departure to Urumqi is now ready for boarding.**

WEI, DINA say goodbye to KEN, JAHID.

SCENE 15

June 2008. Running sequence. China. Chinese music. KEN runs with the flame towards Khotan, south of the Taklamakan desert.

KEN: (*Voiceover.*) **In the River Sien, there are many humming serpents, they are shaped like snakes but have four wings. Three hundred leagues further west there are poisonous eels shaped like yellow snakes, as they move there are flashes of light. Wherever they appear, that place will be struck by severe drought...**

SCENE 16

June 2008. Southern fringes of the Taklamakan. KEN and JAHID have set up camp for the night. Moonlight. JAHID is cooking. KEN is standing with a local WOMAN. She hands him a small package.

KEN: **Thank you.**

The WOMAN exits.

That's so kind.

JAHID: What is it?

KEN: Goat's cheese.

KEN is staring into the distance.

You'd never know.

JAHID: You'd never know what?

KEN: That there were hundreds of square miles of sand out there.

JAHID: Take a look in the morning when the sun comes up.

KEN: You know what I mean. It's vast this...this...

JAHID: Desert?

KEN: We take so much for granted. Don't you think? But I… I see how some of the people live in the places we've been to and… They've got nothing. If I want a pint of milk I go round the corner to Costcutter. And I moan every step of the way 'cos it means I have to leave my books for five minutes to do it. These people want something… That woman… I get pissed off if there isn't a train on the Victoria Line for more than five minutes. She told me she walks ten miles to work every day, and then walks ten miles back. And the people in my block of flats are so… they never look you in the eye, we never speak, but she was all, have a drink, have something to eat. What's wrong with us? People here don't look at you like you're about to stab them… I'm ranting. Is it ready yet?

JAHID: Nearly. I'm sick of noodles.

KEN: Tough.

JAHID: They're like spaghetti gone wrong.

KEN: I'm pretty sure noodles were invented before spaghetti… I want to do at least twenty miles tomorrow. Twenty-six if I can.

JAHID: If it's as hot as it was today you / won't manage…

KEN: We'll need to get more water.

JAHID: Okay.

KEN: How much do you think we'll raise?

JAHID: Don't know.

KEN: What was it the last time you checked?

JAHID: Not a lot of internet cafés around here.

KEN: In Kashgar. At the airport, after Wei and Dina left.

JAHID doesn't answer.

Jahid?

JAHID: Yes?

KEN: How much was it?

No answer.

Jahid?

JAHID: I don't know.

KEN: Why don't you know?

JAHID: I didn't check.

KEN: You always check.

JAHID: It had gone down a bit.

KEN: Gone down? How –

JAHID: Not much.

KEN: How can it go down? You can't un-sponsor someone.

Pause.

Jahid?

JAHID: What?

KEN: How can it go down?

JAHID: I don't know. I'll get the / plates...

KEN: Tell me what's going on.

JAHID: Some people have withdrawn their money.

KEN: How? They can't do that!

JAHID: They...found out...stuff...

KEN: They found out what stuff?

JAHID: I don't know.

KEN: What stuff?

JAHID: That we drove quite a bit of the way.

KEN: How did they know? How…? Jahid –

JAHID: I put it in the blog. And that we used sponsorship money to pay for things.

KEN: You…? Why?

JAHID: I…just did, that's all.

KEN: Why?

JAHID: Dina said I should tell the truth.

KEN: Don't blame Dina.

JAHID: I'm not.

KEN: Shit! Shit-shit-shit! How much have we lost?

JAHID: About six grand. So far. Sorry.

KEN: Why didn't you tell me?

JAHID: It was just after Dina got out of hospital –

KEN: I want you to go.

JAHID: Don't be stupid. You can't stay out here / on your own…

KEN suddenly goes for JAHID. They fight until they are exhausted. JAHID exits.

KEN: Jahid…

JAHID has gone.

Shit…

KEN pulls his sleeping bag around his shoulders and sits staring after JAHID for a moment. Beat. KEN lies down. He tosses and turns. Silence as KEN drifts off to sleep. Lights dim. After a moment we hear a humming sound.
There is an electric flash in the darkness, followed by another flash, and another. The flashes of light momentarily illuminate a vast number (as many as we can manage) of snakes and eels as they slither over KEN's sleeping body. A flash of light illuminates XI standing

in a green dress with her arm aloft, the sleeve of her dress covering her face. A flash of light reveals XI with her arm down – her face is horribly burned and disfigured. KEN screams. Darkness. KEN switches his torch on. XI and the snakes have vanished.

SCENE 17

June 2008. Music. KEN runs alone, alternative Olympic torch in hand, a rucksack on his back. Sound of the wind.

KEN: I'm running through this sand, on this cracked and parched earth. Along this ridge. Beneath this sun. This burning, mid-summer sun…

KEN stops. He stares out over the desert for a moment. It is very hot. He wipes away the sweat, takes a drink of water, then turns and continues running. The sound of the wind intensifies.

I'm running past sand drifts. Through this desolate place. Through this hot wind, this wind that picks up the sand and throws it in my face. Through this sandstorm. This sand obscuring my vision, in my eyes, in my mouth…

The sandstorm intensifies. KEN tries to keep running, but it is difficult. The sand storm howls and swirls, it almost engulfs KEN, slowing him down almost to standing.

XI: (*Voice off.*) **Help…**

KEN: (*Shouting above the storm.*) Xi! Xi, is that you?

XI: (*Voice off.*) **Help me…**

KEN struggles towards the voice. The storm intensifies.

KEN: Xi!!!

XI: (*Voice off.*) **Help…**

*KEN collapses. He is engulfed and buried by sand. The wind stills. The storm relents. A single sun blazes in the sky.
NÜ CH'OU chih shih enters.*

NÜ CHOU: (*Spoken.*) **I am Nü Ch'ou chih shih. I lost my way in the sandstorm. To escape the lacerating sand, I began to climb. I climbed and climbed, until I was high above the land. From the mountain I watched the sand swirl like a child's spinning top below me, spinning away into the distance. Then a quiet, a calm descended.**

> (*Lyric.*) **One sun in the sky**
> **Plentiful Fresh water**
> **The Earth is warm and calm.**

A second sun rises in the sky, borne up on the back of a black crow.[1]
The stage grows brighter.

> (*Lyric.*) **Two suns in the sky**
> **Workers doze in the fields**
> **Too tired now to till**
> **Rice wilts its yield.**

A third sun rises in the sky, borne up on the back of a black crow. The stage grows brighter.

> (*Lyric.*) **Three suns in the sky**
> **People crowd in the shade.**

A fourth sun rises in the sky, born up on the back of a black crow. The stage grows brighter.
The fourth sun is quickly followed by a fifth, sixth and seventh sun. With each sun the stage grows a little brighter.

> (*Lyric.*) **Four suns, oceans rise**
> **Five suns, creatures die**
> **Six suns, whirlwind swirl**
> **Seven suns, world war unfurl.**

An eighth sun rises in the sky.
Part of a snake appears.

> (*Lyric.*) **Eight suns, poison water.**

---

1 According to solar myth the ten suns were borne up into the sky on the back of a black crow.

Part of chisel-tooth appears.

> (*Lyric.*) **Nine suns, poison land.**

A tenth sun rises in the sky.
Part of a giant locust appears.

> (*Lyric.*) **Ten suns**
> **Incinerated where we stand.**

XI removes the sleeve of her dress – her face is horribly disfigured. She collapses. The sand where KEN was buried begins to heave, but it is not KEN who emerges, it is YI the Archer.[1]

YI: (*Spoken.*) **Nü Ch'ou chih shih, do not die. I am Yi the Archer. I will save you. I will shoot down nine of the ten suns...**

YI takes aim at one of the suns. YI fires his arrow. He hits the sun. The sun squeals and hisses as it falls to earth and sinks into the sea. He shoots down a second sun. It falls to earth.

(*Spoken.*) I will slay the creatures of the drought...

The Nine-Gullet Giant-Head Snake[2] *enters. YI and the Nine-Gullet Giant-Head Snake fight. YI is victorious. YI shoots down a third, fourth and fifth sun. Chisel Tooth*[3] *enters. YI and the beast do battle. YI is victorious. YI shoots down a sixth, seventh and eighth sun. The Locust Plague Beast*[4] *enters. YI and the beast do battle. YI is victorious. YI shoots down the ninth sun.*
He kneels at NÜ CH'OU's side.

> (*Lyric.*) **One sun in the sky**
> **One sun up on high.**
> **Nü Ch'ou chih shih**
> **The world is saved**

---

1 Ho Yi God of solar myth. His function was to avert world catastrophe by shooting down the ten suns when they all appeared in the sky together
2 Mythical creature said to have been slain by Yi the Archer.
3 Mythical creature said to have been slain by Yi the Archer.
4 Mythical creature said to have been slain by Yi the Archer.

**Nine suns destroyed
Three beasts slayed.**

**You must rise again
You must find rebirth
You must lead the way
You must restore this earth.**

NÜ CH'OU sits up, re-born. Her face no longer scarred. The sand dunes shift and change shape. YI and NÜ CH'OU disappear beneath the sand. The sand where KEN was buried starts to shift and KEN re-emerges. He crawls a few feet on hands and knees.

KEN: Xi… Where are you?

*KEN collapses. Two Chinese TRADERS enter.
They cross to where KEN has collapsed.*

CHINESE MAN 1: **Is he all right?**

CHINESE MAN 2: **I think so.**

CHINESE MAN 1: **Who is he?**

CHINESE MAN 2: **I don't know. I've never seen him before. Give him some water.**

CHINESE MAN 1 gives KEN some water.

KEN: Xi… Please…

CHINESE MAN 2: **What did he say?**

CHINESE MAN 1: **I don't know.**

CHINESE MAN 2: **It's hot. We should get him into the shade. Help me lift him. Quickly.**

CHINESE MAN 1 lifts KEN onto his back.

This way.

They exit.

SCENE 18

September 2008. The Beijing Olympic Stadium, the Bird's Nest. Early morning. A Rainbow Bird kite in the sky. KEN enters; tired, dirty, his clothes and rucksack threadbare. He stares up at the huge stadium. He laughs quietly to himself. He takes the torch from his rucksack. He tries to turn it on. It won't work. KEN shakes his head. He smiles ruefully to himself. KEN's mobile rings. He answers it.

KEN: Yes… You!… I'm in Beijing… I'm not lying. I'm standing outside the Olym –… I'm not lying… The Bird's Nest…I'm standing right in front of it… Yes, I know the Olympics ended last month. Thanks for–… I'm standing right outside it!

JAHID enters, talking on his mobile.

JAHID: You're lying…

KEN: I'm not –

KEN turns to see JAHID. They smile. They embrace.

JAHID: You know you've still raised quite a bit.

KEN: Yes?

JAHID: Yes. Your exploits are an internet phenomenon. Thanks to me posting your text messages on my blog.

KEN: It's good to see you.

JAHID: You too. There's a couple of your mates here.

DINA and WEI enter. They greet KEN warmly.

KEN: Are you –

DINA: I'm fine. How are you?

KEN: All right.

WEI: Congratulations.

DINA: **Congratulations.**

KEN: You speak Mandarin?

DINA: About four words so far.

JAHID: Did you know that statistically speaking for every mile you jog, you add one minute to your life.

KEN: You reckon?

JAHID: Yes.

KEN: So if I keep running, I'll never die.

JAHID: Yes.

KEN: So you've discovered the secret of immortality?

JAHID: Yes.

KEN: The man's a genius.

XI enters. KEN and XI look at one another for a moment.

XI: So…

KEN: So…

XI: You're here.

KEN: … Yes…

The End.